3 MINUTES TO ARRIVAL

TRINA BELL

Contents

Dedication

This book is dedicated to my mom Cynthia Bell for birthing a champ giving me this gift to share with others (men). My better half Freedell Benton III, he is the reason I even thought of *3minutestoarrival* because he gave me the name and it was through this I derived the motivation for compiling this book. They are my biggest fans and the source of my determination to move forward. Also I want to thank my friends and family for pushing me and encouraging me to follow my dream. Indeed, life is easier when you are surrounded with the right people by your side urging you on every step of the way.

Preface

Man is a sexual being. We are all in one way or the other in the pursuit of happiness. One of the mediums through which adults derive happiness is through the instrumentality of sex; this is why when there is lack of sexual satisfaction in a relationship, there tends to be dissatisfaction and unhappiness in such relationship. As humans, the desire to engage in sex is a feeling that comes upon everyone, sometimes during the years of puberty, and endures for many years mostly till late adulthood. Just like we naturally need to eat, there is a natural need for sex for most human being. Women and Gays for several centuries have been inhibited in expressing themselves in the act of sex because society prefers them to be submissive in everything, but the tide has turned. Woman, you can dominate your man in the bedroom. You possess the key to stimulating him and making him do your bidding in the bedroom. This book is loaded with actionable tips through which you can boost your sexual experience with your partner and take it all to a whole new level.

Introduction

Just when you thought you can do it all, permit me to reveal some deep secrets of oral sex to you.

Let Trina teach you balls and all. Who says you can't be in control? The human body operates like a reservoir of water with a tap acting as the control switch. This tap in the male body is the penis. When you can control it well, you will be able to control the level of pleasure your partner feels during sexual activity. 3 minutes to arrival, I'll help you get there. No standby no cancellations! Let Trina guide you to your destination. This book will help you discover the power you never thought you had. Please note that in this book the act of oral sex is sometimes illustrated as a plane taking off at the airport and traveling towards another. This is what each chapter of this book is illustrated after.

CHECK-IN

The act of sex involves an intense feeling of pleasure between the partners engaging in the act. Three minutes to arrival i.e. ejaculation can be pleasing to any man. The feeling is so enthralling and highly stimulating, it is almost impossible to describe it. It is as if the body is being ravished with multiple bouts of pleasure at the same time. However, many do not get to enjoy the sweet sensations and pleasures that comes with sex because they just cannot 'stay up' for up to a minute or two before reaching orgasm and ejaculating. Sex is best enjoyed when each of the partners stay long enough to please their partners; this is why sex should not last for too long neither should it be too short as well because if it is too short, it can lead to lack of satisfaction of at least one of the parties and can ultimately lead them to explore other means of sexual satisfaction.

The pertinent question to ask then is what is the minimum time for a round of sex to last? I would readily say there is no universal answer to this as human differences do apply, hence what works for couple A might not work for couple B. However, I would like to say that a round of sex should not be any less than three minutes regardless of the situation or condition. There is one important thing most people are unaware of though and I have found that ignorance of this knowledge has severely affected the relationships of many around. Many women do not know that they can determine and control when their men orgasm or ejaculate! Yes, this is possible. The maxim "Girl Power" has not been any more apt than in the act of sex. You literally hold the switch to his DICK and you need to use it to your satisfaction. They say knowledge is power and ignorance is weakness, permit me to guide you on how to help your man last longer and please you more in the bedroom. Are you ready? Let's go!

o·ral sex

/ˈôrəl,ˈōrəl seks/

noun

> sexual activity in which the genitals of one partner are stimulated by the mouth of the other; fellatio or cunnilingus.

The first thing to do is to get yourself into position i.e. a comfortable space and posture convenient for sex. Do you like getting down on your knees, laying down or do you prefer sitting in a chair, bar stool, high chair or need something to prop yourself in the back? Are you a lazy D.S (dick sucker)? Do you want to be lying off the bed sideways on the sofa or are you in a back seat or front seat of a vehicle? Are you outside in a public area like movie theatre, mall, bathroom, gas station, red light stop sign, bowling alley, hotel, park, friend's house, cousin house or on a holiday or in the privacy of your own home, wherever you are, make sure your position is comfortable for the next 3 minutes because even if your partner is great with sex but you are in a difficult and uncomfortable posture then you can be sure that the sex will not be very enjoyable; your partner might be enjoying it but you will just be feeling the pain alone. This is a serious issue that has become the undoing of many couples for long. Posture is like the template from which sex must be served.

Many women do prefer to lie down; I don't know why, but this seems like the most common posture for sex. If you want to be lying down you will need to grab the penis with two hands only to guide the strokes and the pace and/or speed of the penis (you are in control). I don't like monotony and I do prefer that partners experiment when engaging in sexual intercourse. However, in lying down or in any posture you so choose, please ensure you are comfortable. While lying down, you are to grab the penis with your two hands to stimulate it and rev it up like you would rev the engine of a car that has not be driven for long to action. If you don't like the scrotum-nuts, ball sack hairballs etc. in your face I suggest you sit in an upward position. I do recommend kneeling position if you truly want to stimulate and arouse your partner orally before the main action. Stimulation is like the first course that will prepare the ground for the main sex which is the main dish. Kneeling is preferred because when you are on your knees you have full control of the penis and you are able to look the man right in the face and let him know you mean business. Exchanging glances at this point further drives up the appetite for sex and makes him want to devour you.

Hygiene

Hygiene is very important to sex. It has a direct connection to libido! Before you open your mouth, if you smell anything that smell a little foul, like if you smell a scent of musk or anything out of the ordinary, get up and change flights, that plane needs attention and is certainly not ready boarding yet. Many couples speak about their partner's reluctance to go the extra mile on the field of play whenever it is time to get it on. They often think of every other thing being the issue except bad smell. The truth is that the brain controls every activity of the body, whenever you smell a foul smell during sex; it could send a message to your brain which could then communicate to your penis that it is time to disengage. This could be the reason many flights get interrupted and have to be canceled in the bedroom.

BOARDING

As a woman, you have to know your way around the penis of your partner. See yourself as the real owner, after all his penis is there for your pleasure. Examine his penis regularly; rub it and caress it, massage and tickle it and you could lick it as well. Whatever you do with his penis just don't start right off sucking the penis. This is because it is good that you tease the penis and get it ready for your mouth; jumpstart the penis and show the penis who is boss! Grab that penis with 1 hand and gently lather it up them lips and make sure you get that tongue ready for takeoff because when the plane takes off, it's going to be ferocious.

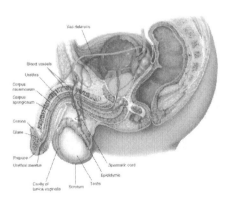

As you begin to suck, your main focus is the tip of the penis or head; you start off by kissing the tip in order to get it wet. In order for you to suck it well, you can imagine the tip of the penis are lips that you are merely kissing with your tongue! Give it several licks and kisses concurrently; by this time the penis should have gotten an erection, when it is hard and standing tall like a soldier obeying the clarion call to duty. From here, you then work your way down to the rest of the penis area. If the measurements of the penis is short then your arrival will be clear and ready for landing, if the measurements of the penis is a lil longer then the trip might seem a lil longer; either way the journey will be fun. If the passenger wants you to buckle up (i.e. use a condom), you will have to apply a little bit more pressure to get through the latex; same strategy same route just more luggage with the seatbelt on (condom). You can use a little teeth, and when I say teeth I mean when you are tongue-kissing and licking the tip, as you pull away from the tip you want to snug the belt (condom) with a little teeth so that the passenger can know you are a beast. The belt (condom) is great when its time to land, if you are grossed out about semen nut or you are not a swallower; the seatbelt is perfect in this scenario. There are some that claims they don't like condom because it does not give the same sensation with skin to skin sex but hey, if you don't like nut on you, you want to prevent pregnancy or want to be safe cos you are not sure of your partner's status, then it is best you go with condom.

Sucking the D is a skill you must have as a woman. You do not have to be a deep throater, you do not have to place the full penis in your mouth, you don't have to swallow the penis, NO but if you can then great, that's extra, you are headhunter #1.

Start off with enough spit to cover the tip of the penis (if you don't like a lot of spit or if you don't like the smell or feeling then place a tasty treat in your mouth before you start)

Suggestive treats: mints (small)

Now and later (chewable) 1 piece

Gum (flavor) half a strip

Peppermints (puff)

Fruit roll up (small piece)

Powdered candy

Spray candy or

Any type of flavor-able candy that dissolves in the mouth that you don't have to chew.

The essence is for you to be motivated in sucking his dick because that is what injects life into it and gets it ready for action. Please be mindful, if you can't multitask (keep candy on the tongue and suck) please don't use any of these treats. This is important in order for you to prevent choking during takeoff.

TAKEOFF

Once you get the tip all lathered up, now it's time to move on to the penis; by this time, you are 1 minute in time to takeoff. You will take your tongue in a vertical motion moving it at a high speed. Your tongue will be on the raft of the penis, at this time the penis should by lifted upward in the air while your hand is in a circular motion on the tip (the whole time your hand that is on the tip of the penis caressing it, it should be wet and never dry) while the penis is upward, this gives you access to the balls, if you are a baller you will need to put as much spit as you can stand on the balls, you will inhale the balls in one deep breath and suck really gentle, don't try to put both balls (sack) in your mouth because there is really no need to show-off now. Move your way back up to the tip where you would then go now in a really fast motion; if the penis is hard, your main focus on the tip is the cuff under the tip, take your tongue and go round and round and suck the tip after each lick.

ARRIVAL

2 minutes into action, his toes are curling up, he's gripping your head and hair really tight. Moaning from both parties are getting louder and louder as you now have him totally at your service. If your hands are still caressing the balls, you will feel a tight sensation as the passenger is obviously nearing arrival at this time. If the seat belt is still on; great, just continue to keep sucking until you feel a warm gush hit your tongue. Gently slide his penis in and out of your mouth. Start from the head downwards. Gradually slide him deeper and deeper into your mouth as much of him you can accommodate. As the man, he will have firsthand information about when he's feeling like cumming. He will inform you and you can then decide whether you want to swallow or not. If you are a swallower, as the arrival is approaching, get ready for clearance once the semen (nut) enters your mouth wait until the passenger is completely done before swallowing, you will hold the semen in your

mouth until he clarifies it's over, swallowing too fast will cause some gagging and or chocking. If you are a spitter, let the passenger know ahead of time so he will pull out of your mouth to arrive, or once he arrives, you will hold the semen in your mouth and find a safe place to spit it out. At that, this concludes the 3 minutes to arrival. At this point, the plane has landed and the passengers have disengaged and checked in.

TIPS

- If you are in take-off stage and you feel the arrival will take longer than 3 minutes, lather the penis up and hop on it, you will ride in a circular motion i.e. up and down really fast. Swerve your body vigorously on it as if you are riding a horse at high speed. Once you feel his moaning and or his body beginning to show signs of incoming release of semen, it's time to hop off his dick and get ready for arrival

- Always go head 1st. It is an unwritten rule that, to get the best out of sex, you need to give him so good a blowjob! This is like a test drive to get the plane ready for the flight that is about to happen.

- Never force the time, if you are the best it will arrive 3 minutes or less. Focus on yourself because if you are good, your partner will find a way to measure up to standard as well.

- Never let the passenger feel your teeth. Never! The sexual organs of both males and females are soft and tender and might get easily bruised in the event of close contact between it and the penis. Nothing kills sexual mood as fast as the scrape of teeth around the tender parts of the penis.

- Making noise (moaning), and looking directly in the eyes of the beholder is always good. Make sure you moan at intervals because moaning makes him feel good, it motivates him to do more to please you. This is important because it takes two to tangle and sex is best enjoyed when the two parties are willing to go at it. In this light, making noise during sex encourages your partner to go faster.

- It's better to give than to receive. The more you please your man, the more he is motivated to please you too.

- If your neck or mouth gets tired, use your hand for backup (grip tight and move accordingly) he will never know you have withdrawn your mouth.

- Before arriving at the airport do mouth exercises, open and shut your mouth like 5 times, close the mouth then place lips together as if you are about to kiss and move up and down side to side. This action increases the sensitivity around his penis and therefore heightens his pleasure.

- No matter the size you are headhunter #1

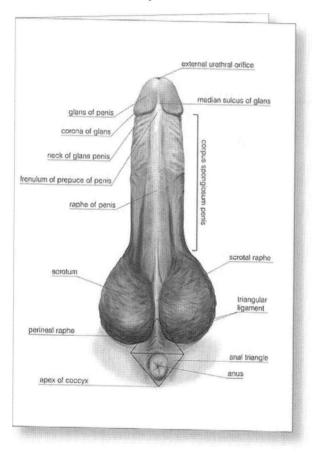

POINTERS

Every time you spit, make sure it's straight on the dick. This is to keep it moist and to maintain its sensitivity. You are in control, how you handle the penis can determine how long it stays erect or goes limp. You can decide to fold and make that penis stand tall by sucking it until it falls 3 minutes or less. Damn! The rest Trina will teach you, Trina will bless you, never use teeth, suck it as if it was a piece of beef, as if you are teethless and you licking a lollipop. If you don't eat meat, suck it like a sweet treat, Lick lick lick if it doesn't work, then stick stick stick.

About the author

Passionate about her craft which is sex therapy; Trina has a passion for helping and is satisfied as people achieve the utmost sexual satisfaction possible in their relationships. She specializes in unraveling the techniques of oral sex because she believes this is the key to a lasting and enjoyable sexual experience. Her interest in oral sex developed long ago when her mom implored her to 'use her mouth for meaningful things other than talking nonsense' and this she did at a young age when she started to be sexually active and this led her to discover oral sex with her 32 sexual partners, a handful of which can tell you her mouth is the truth! She has shared her mouth with several men before now; now let Trina teach you what your mouth can do!

I want you to achieve 3 minutes or less but understand that 3 minutes of pleasure can give you a lifetime of pain, practice safe sex at all times.

Made in the USA
Monee, IL
18 April 2022

94165516R00015